It's My State!

NEW YORK

The Empire State

Dan Elish and Stephanie Fitzgerald

Cavendish Square

New York

Published in 2015 by Cavendish Square Publishing, LLC
243 5th Avenue, Suite 136, New York, NY 10016

Copyright © 2015 by Cavendish Square Publishing, LLC

Third Edition

Website: cavendishsq.com

This publication represents the opinions and views of the author based on his or her personal experience, knowledge, and research. The information in this book serves as a general guide only. The author and publisher have used their best efforts in preparing this book and disclaim liability rising directly or indirectly from the use and application of this book.

CPSIA Compliance Information: Batch #WS14CSQ

All websites were available and accurate when this book was sent to press.

Library of Congress Cataloging-in-Publication Data
Elish, Dan.
 New York / Dan Elish, Stephanie Fitzgerald. — Third edition.
    pages cm. — (It's my state)
 Includes index.
 ISBN 978-1-62712-752-3 (hardcover) ISBN 978-1-62712-753-0 (ebook)
 1. New York (State)—Juvenile literature. I. Fitzgerald, Stephanie. II. Title.

 F119.3.E37 2015
 974.7—dc23

 2014007421

Editorial Director: Dean Miller
Editor, Third Edition: Nicole Sothard
Art Director: Jeffrey Talbot
Series Designer, Third Edition: Jeffrey Talbot
Layout Design, Third Edition: Erica Clendening
Production Manager: Jennifer Ryder-Talbot

The photographs in this book are used by permission and through the courtesy of: Cover Inigo Cia/Moment/Getty Images; pp. 4 (top), 4 (middle), 4 (bottom), 5 (top), 5 (middle), 5 (bottom), 8, 9, 12, 14 (middle), 14 (bottom), 15 (middle), 15 (bottom), 17, 18, 19, 20 (top), 20 (middle), 20 (bottom), 21 (top), 21 (middle), 21 (bottom), 34 (top), 34 (middle), 34 (bottom), 35 (top), 35 (middle), 48 (bottom), 51, 53, 54 (top), 56, 67, 68 (top), 69 (top), 70 Shutterstock.com; p. 6 Mitchell Funk/Getty Images; p. 11 (bottom) Richard Cavalleri/Shutterstock.com; p. 13 Courtesy of NASA's Earth Observatory; p. 14 (top) Jorg Hackemann/Shutterstock.com; p. 15 (top) Aspen Photos/Shutterstock.com; p. 16 AFP/Getty Images; pp. 22, 27, 33, 41, 44, 47 (bottom) Archive Photos/Getty Images; p. 24 Getty Images; p. 28 Frank Paul/Alamy; p. 29 Northwind Picture Archives; p. 32 Universal Images Group/Getty Images; p. 35 (bottom) © Matt H. Wade via Wikimedia Commons; pp. 37, 38, 39, 47 (top), 49 (bottom) Hulton Archive/Getty Images; p. 40 photo.ua/Shutterstock.com; pp. 48 (top), 49 (middle) Helga Esteb/Shutterstock.com; p. 48 (middle) JStone/Shutterstock.com; p. 49 (top) landmarkmedia/Shutterstock.com; p. 54 (middle) kezee/Flickr; p. 54 (bottom) Enoch Ross/Flickr; p. 55 (top) Scott Cornell/Shutterstock.com; p. 55 (middle) Twitch/Flickr; p. 55 (bottom) Sebastian Barre/Flickr; pp. 59, 62 (top) NY Daily News via Getty Images; p. 60 Visions of America, LLC/Alamy; p. 62 (middle) Time & Life Pictures/Getty Images; p. 62 (bottom) J Carter Rinaldi/Getty Images; p. 63 Sean Gallup/Getty Images; p. 64 Robnroll/Shutterstock.com; p. 68 (middle) Mint Images, Bill Miles/Getty Images; p. 69 (middle) Bloomberg via Getty Images; p. 69 (bottom) Spencer Platt/Getty Images; p. 75 (top) Chris Murray/Getty Images; p. 75 (middle) Panoramic Images/Getty Images; p. 75 (bottom) Raymond Gehman/National Geographic/Getty Images.

Printed in the United States of America

NEW YORK
CONTENTS

State Tree: Sugar Maple

Known primarily for producing the sap that makes maple syrup, the sugar maple is also one of the world's most beautiful trees. Each fall its changing leaves paint the New York landscape in brilliant shades of gold, orange, and red.

State Bird: Bluebird

The bluebird was made the state bird in 1970. Many people hang special nesting boxes on fences to attract these pretty, sweet-sounding birds, which winter throughout the state.

State Flower: Rose

Although New York started the state flower movement in the late 1800s, the rose was not officially picked as New York's state flower until 1955. This beautiful and fragrant flower, which has more than 150 species and more than 20,000 hybrids, seems a fitting choice to represent such a diverse state.

NEW YORK

State Animal: Beaver

Although adopted as the state animal only in 1975, the beaver played an important part in New York's history. In the 1600s, fur traders bartered with Native Americans for beaver pelts, which they sold to European merchants. This led many traders to settle near Albany, now the state's capital.

State Beverage: Milk

Milk was named the state beverage in 1981. It must have been an easy choice, since dairy farming is one of New York's most important industries. It takes about two days for a quart of New York milk to get from the cow (where it comes out at 101 degrees Fahrenheit, or 38 degrees Celsius) to the grocery store.

State Fish: Brook Trout

Found in the lakes of the Adirondack Mountains, as well as in hundreds of streams throughout the state, the brook trout was named New York's freshwater fish in 1975.

The Empire State Building in New York City is one of the most famous symbols of New York State.

The Empire State

During the height of the American Revolution, General George Washington toured the New York colony. According to legend, the future president declared that New York would one day become the seat of an **empire**. The "Empire State" was a land of forests and mountains, but, over time, Washington was proved right. A century later, New York City had become the financial center of North America. A bit farther upstate, lumberjacks and farmers kept pace, producing timber and raising livestock and crops.

Today, New York is home to more than 19 million people, making it the third most populous state in the nation, after California and Texas.

New York State is known for its diversity. Walk down any street in New York City, Buffalo, or Albany. You will see people of many different nationalities. The people are what make this state great.

New York's diversity is not limited to its people, though. Whether you enjoy the hustle and bustle of a big city or a peaceful life in the mountains, this state has something for everyone.

Let's learn more about New York. It is not quite an "empire," but its unique blend of big cities, thriving suburbs, quiet countryside, and interesting people have turned it into a dynamic state.

The Hudson River flows south for more than 300 miles (500 km) from the Adirondack Mountains to New York City.

New York Borders	
North:	Canada
	Lake Ontario
South:	New Jersey
	Pennsylvania
East:	Vermont
	Massachusetts
	Connecticut
West:	Canada
	Lake Erie
	Pennsylvania

The Landscape

Driving on the bustling avenues of New York City or even along the quiet roads of the more rural areas, it is hard to imagine that the landscape was formed more than one million years ago during one of Earth's Ice Ages. That is when a huge glacier, towering higher than the Empire State Building, moved across the state and carved out the Finger Lakes, the Hudson River Valley, and the valleys of the Adirondacks. It also created Long Island.

At 47,224 square miles (122,310 square kilometers), New York is the 30th largest state in land area and is often divided into seven regions. Hugging the Saint Lawrence River in the northeastern section of the state is the flat terrain and rich soil of the Saint Lawrence Lowland. Farther south, the majestic Adirondack Mountains rise in a region called the Adirondack Upland. This is wonderful "outdoors" country, where New Yorkers can visit any of more than 2,000 lakes or go skiing at one of the area's famous resorts, such as Lake Placid and Gore and Whiteface mountains. The highlight of a visit would include seeing Mount Marcy, which at 5,344 feet (1,629 meters), is New York's highest peak.

South of the Adirondacks lies the Hudson-Mohawk Lowland, which contains some of the most fertile farmland in the country. The Hudson and Mohawk rivers flow through the region, which includes winding country roads, solitary creeks, and small farms and towns. The New England Upland sits to the east of the Hudson River along the Taconic Mountains, and the Atlantic Coastal Plain stretches across the southeastern section of the state. This region includes Long Island and the state's beachfront areas along Long Island Sound and the Atlantic Ocean.

The Appalachian Plateau is the largest of the Empire State's seven regions. The Finger Lakes and some of New York's most lovely scenery are here. Known for its flat expanses and beautiful snowy winters, this region has small towns and dairy farms but few cities. The Great Lakes Lowland fills most of the northwestern section of the state. This is where Oneida Lake is found as well as three of the state's major cities: Syracuse, Rochester, and Buffalo. The beautiful coasts of Lakes Erie and Ontario are also in this region, not to mention one of the most astounding natural wonders in all of America: Niagara Falls.

Whiteface Mountain, the fifth highest peak in the Adirondacks, is a popular skiing destination.

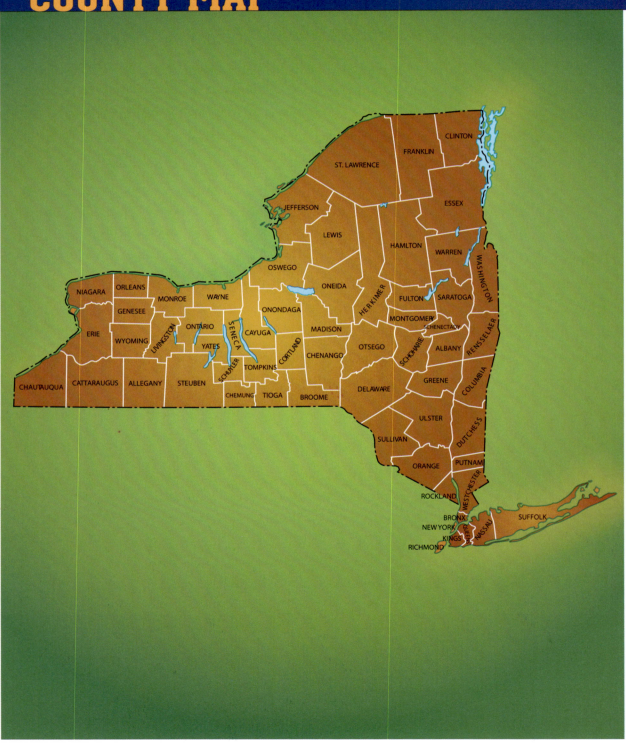

NEW YORK
POPULATION BY COUNTY

County	Population	County	Population	County	Population
Albany County	304,204	Monroe County	744,344	Tompkins County	101,564
Allegany County	48,946	Montgomery County	50,219	Ulster County	182,493
Bronx County	1,385,108	Nassau County	1,339,532	Warren County	65,707
Broome County	200,600	New York County	1,585,873	Washington County	63,216
Cattaraugus County	80,317	Niagara County	216,469	Wayne County	93,772
Cayuga County	80,026	Oneida County	234,878	Westchester County	949,113
Chautauqua County	134,905	Onondaga County	467,026	Wyoming County	42,155
Chemung County	88,830	Ontario County	107,931	Yates County	25,348
Chenango County	50,477	Orange County	372,813		
Clinton County	82,128	Orleans County	42,883		
Columbia County	63,096	Oswego County	122,109		
Cortland County	49,336	Otsego County	62,259		
Delaware County	47,980	Putnam County	99,710		
Dutchess County	297,488	Queens County	2,230,722		
Erie County	919,040	Rensselaer County	159,429		
Essex County	39,370	Richmond County	468,730		
Franklin County	51,599	Rockland County	311,687		
Fulton County	55,531	Saratoga County	219,607		
Genesee County	60,079	Schenectady County	154,727		
Greene County	49,221	Schoharie County	32,749		
Hamilton County	4,836	Schuyler County	18,343		
Herkimer County	64,519	Seneca County	35,251		
Jefferson County	116,229	Steuben County	98,990		
Kings County	2,504,700	St. Lawrence County	111,944		
Lewis County	27,087	Suffolk County	1,493,350		
Livingston County	65,393	Sullivan County	77,547		
Madison County	73,442	Tioga County	51,125		

Source: U.S. Bureau of the Census, 2010

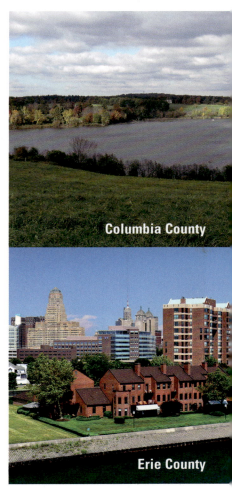

Columbia County

Erie County

The Five Boroughs of New York City

Located in the southeastern corner of the state, New York City, otherwise known as the Big Apple, is not set on one piece of land. Rather, it is a collection of five boroughs—the Bronx, Brooklyn, Manhattan, Queens, and Staten Island—that are partly on the mainland and partly on islands in or facing New York Harbor. The boroughs are connected by roads, bridges, and tunnels.

The island of Manhattan is 13.4 miles (21.5 km) long and 2.3 miles (3.7 km) wide at its widest point. It is only 0.8 miles (1.3 km) wide at its narrowest point. Manhattan is where you can find the Wall Street business district, the Empire State Building and many other skyscrapers, Central Park, and the glittering lights of Times Square. A 9-mile (14.5-km) strait known as the East River separates Manhattan from Brooklyn and Queens, which are on the western end of Long Island.

Brooklyn is the most populous and second largest borough. An estimated 2.5 million people live there. Brooklyn is known for its many diverse and ethnic neighborhoods. Brighton Beach has a large Ukrainian and Russian population. Bedford-Stuyvesant is known for its large African American population. Other neighborhoods include Bensonhurst (Italian), Williamsburg (Jewish), and Bushwick (Puerto Rican). Some attractions in Brooklyn include Prospect Park, the Brooklyn Botanic Garden, and Coney Island.

In 2011, Niagara Falls was named the fifth most visited tourist attraction in the world.

The Finger Lakes were formed when glaciers moved through the region millions of years ago. You can see the Finger Lakes in this satellite photo.

Queens is the largest and the second most populous borough. Like Brooklyn, Queens has many neighborhoods that have large ethnic communities. Howard Beach is largely Italian-American, Flushing has a large Asian community, and Astoria has a large Greek population. Queens is home to Citi Field, where the New York Mets play, JFK and LaGuardia airports, and the USTA Billie Jean King National Tennis Center, where the US Open tennis tournament is held every year.

The Bronx, which is located across the Harlem River from Manhattan, is the only borough actually on the U.S. mainland. At 42 square miles (109 sq km), it is the fourth largest borough. The Bronx was once a rural area, but the addition of subway stations and urban sprawl caused population growth there. Yankee Stadium and the Bronx Zoo are two major attractions in the Bronx. Pelham Bay Park, the largest park in New York City, is also located there. Pelham Bay Park is three times the size of Manhattan's Central Park.

Staten Island lies across Upper New York Bay, a short ferry ride from lower Manhattan. It is the third largest and the least populous borough. Staten Island is mostly residential and industrial, however the second largest park in New York City is being built there. Fresh Kills Park was once a landfill, however when it is finished, the park will feature more than 2,000 acres (809 ha) of trails, waterways, and open land for residents and visitors to enjoy.

Besides New York City's five boroughs, the state has 57 other counties, giving New York a total of 62 counties.

10 KEY SITES

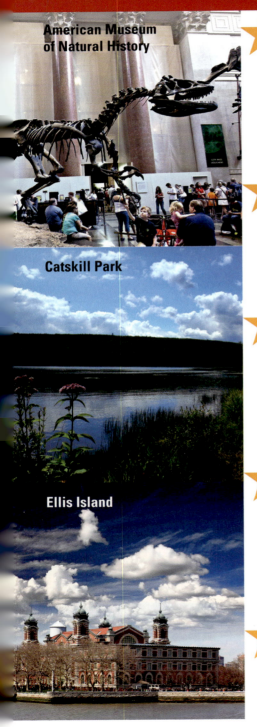

American Museum of Natural History

Catskill Park

Ellis Island

1. Adirondack Park

Adirondack Park covers 6 million acres (2,428,113 ha) of northern New York. It is the largest publicly protected area in the contiguous 48 states. Residents and visitors hike the more than 2,000 miles (3,219 km) of trails, fish its lakes, and enjoy its wildlife.

2. American Museum of Natural History

Located in New York City, the American Museum of Natural History is famous for its scientific and cultural exhibits. These exhibits include plants, animals, artifacts, and dinosaur fossils. Around 5 million people visit the museum every year.

3. Catskill Park

Catskill Park, in southeastern New York, is a popular place to explore the outdoors. Visitors can hike its mountains and fish, swim, and camp. The park is also home to many artists and musicians. People enjoy the many art museums and concerts that take place there.

4. Ellis Island

Ellis Island is a small island in New York Harbor, in New York City. Between 1892 and 1954, Ellis Island was the first stop for more than 12 million **immigrants** who came to America to start a new life. Today, Ellis Island has a museum at which you can learn about the island's important history.

5. Metropolitan Museum of Art

The Metropolitan Museum of Art is the largest art museum in the United States. It includes paintings and sculptures by some of the most famous artists in the world.

NEW YORK

6. National Baseball Hall of Fame and Museum

Cooperstown, New York is home to the National Baseball Hall of Fame and Museum. More than 300,000 people visit each year to learn about the history of baseball and honor their favorite players. The museum is filled with memorabilia and has around 135,000 baseball cards.

7. Niagara Falls

Niagara Falls is the name for three large waterfalls that are located on the border of New York State and Ontario, Canada. They are named Horseshoe Falls, American Falls, and Bridal Veil Falls. About 750,000 gallons of water flow over the falls every second!

8. Saratoga National Historic Park

This historical park near Albany is where American soldiers defeated the British Army in two important battles during the American Revolution, in 1777. Visitors to the park can learn details of the fight and visit the battlefield.

9. The Strong National Museum of Play

The Strong is an educational center in Rochester, New York that studies and celebrates play. The center includes the National Center of Play and the National Toy Hall of Fame. People of all ages can play games, solve puzzles, and see the world's largest toy collection.

10. 1,000 Islands

The 1,000 Islands is an archipelago, or collection of islands, located on the border of northern New York and southeastern Ontario, Canada. The 1,000 Islands is actually made up of 1,864 islands. You can see or visit many of them by ferryboat.

National Baseball Hall of Fame

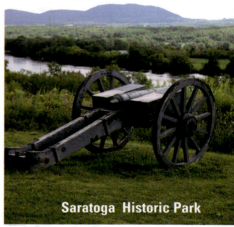

Saratoga Historic Park

1,000 Islands

Climate

New York State has an extremely varied climate. The people of western New York, from Syracuse through Rochester and Buffalo, experience harsh winters like those of Canada to the north. More than 100 inches (254 cm) of snow can fall each winter. It is not uncommon to have 1 to 3 inches (2.5-7.6 cm) of snow fall daily in these areas. The largest snowfall, though, is due to what is called lake-effect snow.

Lake-effect snow is produced when cold winds move across the warmer waters of Lake Erie and Lake Ontario, which produces energy. The resulting water vapor freezes and is deposited in narrow bands of precipitation that slowly move across the region near the lakes. Many inches of snow can fall within hours, making travel dangerous.

Syracuse is often ranked the number one snowiest large city in the United States. Average snowfall there is around 116 inches (295 cm). The snowiest winter in Syracuse was the 1992-

The Adirondacks is a popular place to visit during the winter months. Here a mother and child take a ride down a toboggan slide onto Mirror Lake in Lake Placid.

1993 season, in which 192 inches (488 cm) of snow fell. This was due in part to the Blizzard of 1993, during which Syracuse received 42 inches (107 cm) of snow in two days.

Smaller towns north of Syracuse, however, get even more snow. Over a ten-day period in February 2007, 141 inches (358 cm) of lake-effect snow fell in Redfield, in Oswego County. That is over 11 feet (3.4 m) of snow!

Not that winter is a picnic for those New Yorkers who live farther south and east. Residents of New York City spend a lot of time commuting outside, and that means during the winter as well. Compared to other parts of the state, though, the city's weather is tame. New York City averages only around 25 inches (64 cm) of snow a year, however it is still very cold. As one native of New York City put it, "There's nothing worse than rounding a street corner in the city in January and getting hit head-on by a blast of wind. Talk about cold!"

What about the Adirondacks? Years ago, they were nicknamed America's Siberia. The temperature in the winter can reach into the negative digits. The wind chill often makes the temperature feel even colder. Average snowfall per month is 15 to 20 inches (38-51 cm) during the winter. Skiers and other winter–sports enthusiasts love the Adirondacks because of its cold and snowy weather.

Coney Island, in New York City, is a popular place for people to swim, go on rides, and walk the boardwalk in the summer months.

Of course, New York does have more temperate seasons. In fact, this is one part of the country where people experience the full effect of all four seasons. Autumn is one of the most celebrated seasons. The crisp autumn air comes to the state in September and generally lingers into early November. This is the time to witness the incredible fall foliage for which New York and other northeastern states are famous. The state is located far enough south that spring comes relatively early, with moderate temperatures lasting through June. Beautiful spring blossoms can be seen everywhere—from the busiest roadsides to the quietest lanes. Summers, too, can be extremely pleasant—but sometimes also quite hot. Especially in the lower portions of the state, July and August daytime temperatures can reach the upper 90s Fahrenheit (upper 30s Celsius).

Wildlife

Much has changed in New York State over the past 400 years. When settlers first arrived, the region was covered from end to end with forests and meadows. Today, a great deal of the landscape has been transformed. Cities, towns, factories, and farms cover much of the land.

The wild turkey population declined in the 1840s due to over-farming. However, by the 1940s, old farmland had returned to woodland and brush. Land in New York could once again support a large turkey population.

Otters are often seen looking for fish to eat in New York's rivers and lakes.

Not everything has changed, however. There are still plenty of wild places to be found in New York. New York is home to 7,600 lakes, ponds, and reservoirs, as well as a portion of two of the Great Lakes, and more than 70,000 miles (112,650 km) of rivers and streams flow through the state. More than 60 percent of the land is still covered by forests, which are home to many hundreds of different kinds of plants and animals.

New York has set aside some wonderful places to see all this spectacular wildlife in a natural setting. Among other things, you can look for moose in the Adirondack Mountains, visit the southeastern shore of Lake Ontario to watch raptors make their spring migration, or track deer on Fire Island (off the south shore of Long Island). New York's natural world is managed by a state government agency called the Bureau of Wildlife. It was founded by the state **legislature** in 1895, at a time when wildlife populations were extremely small.

The bureau's mission is to protect New York's animal life. Because of its efforts, species such as the beaver, white-tailed deer, wood duck, bald eagle, peregrine falcon, ruffed grouse, and wild turkey have been brought back from the brink of extinction and are now often seen in New York forests, fields, and waterways.

No doubt about it: there is more to New York than busy cities. One of the Empire State's greatest assets is its animal life.

Apple Tree

Bluebird

Ladybug

1. Apple Tree

New York is the second largest apple-producing state in the United States. It averages 29.5 million bushels (898,596 cubic meters) annually. The top 3 apple varieties grown are McIntosh, Empire, and Red Delicious.

2. State Animal: Beaver

The beaver is recognizable by its large body and flat tail. The beaver's tail helps it swim New York's many streams, ponds, and marshes. Beavers eat the branches, leaves, and bark of woody plants.

3. State Bird: Bluebird

Male bluebirds are bright blue with white undersides and orange-brown breasts. Females are gray-blue. Bluebirds eat insects, such as beetles and crickets, which they can spot from 100 feet (30 m) away. They also eat berries and wild fruit.

4. State Fish: Brook Trout

The brook trout is one of the most popular fish in New York State. It often looks different depending on where it's found. In streams, trout are sometimes brown or dark green with spots or lines. In lakes, trout are often silver.

5. State Insect: Ladybug

The nine-spotted ladybug is New York's state insect. It is red with nine black spots. This ladybug was thought to be extinct since 1982, however it was rediscovered in 2011.

6. Red Fox

The red fox can be found in almost every county in New York. It has a red coat with a white underside and black legs and ears. Red foxes eat small mammals and birds.

7. State Flower: Rose

Wild roses tend to have just five petals. Roses that are cultivated, or grown by people, have many more petals. Roses come in many different colors, including red, pink, yellow, and white.

8. State Tree: Sugar Maple

The sugar maple became New York's state tree in 1956. It is the most common of the seven maple trees found in the state. Sap from the sugar maple is used for maple syrup production, and its wood is used for construction and heating homes.

9. Sweet Corn

Sweet corn is an important plant in New York. It was one of the main crops grown by New York's Native American tribes. Today, corn is still grown in every rural county in the state, and fresh corn is a popular food eaten during the late summer months.

10. White-Tailed Deer

The white-tailed deer is one of the most common animals to see throughout New York State. Adult deer have red-brown coats in the summer and gray-brown coats in the winter. Fawns, or baby deer, are brown with white spots. Deer are most often seen in the early morning and early evening.

Rose

Sweet Corn

White-Tailed Deer

New Amsterdam, a 17th Century Dutch settlement, was located on what is now the southern tip of Manhattan.

From the Beginning

2

The story goes that in 1626 one of the area's early settlers, a Dutchman named Peter Minuit, bought the island of Manhattan for the Dutch West India Company from the Manhatesen people for goods worth about 60 guilders, which was the equivalent of about 24 dollars. No one knows for certain if the story is true, and in any case, Native Americans did not share the European idea that land could be owned by individuals. But if the story is essentially accurate, this was undoubtedly one of the greatest real-estate bargains in history—for New York City has become one of the most valuable pieces of land in the world. Though not all of the decisions made by the settlers of New York have been this profitable, many other New Yorkers have changed the course of history.

Early Settlers

Ten thousand years ago, the region that now includes New York State was populated by hunters who tracked herds of elk and caribou, caught bears, fish, and small mammals, and gathered plants and seeds from the forest. Although archaeologists continue to discover spearheads and stone knives left by those first residents, little is known about them.

The first documented history of the region begins with the Native Americans who were in the area shortly before the arrival of European explorers and settlers. Several tribes of Algonquian-speaking people populated the southeastern part of what is now New York State. They lived along the banks of the lower Hudson River and on Staten Island, Long Island, and Manhattan. They were driven off their land when the Mohawk, Oneida, Onondaga, Cayuga, and Seneca tribes moved south from the forests farther north and overcame them. These five tribes waged fierce wars among themselves until sometime between 1140 and 1600, when they formed the Iroquois **Confederacy**. This was a political organization in which each tribe enjoyed some independence but answered to the authority of the confederacy's Great Council. Most important, the tribes agreed to fight as one and not against each other. At the height of its power, the Iroquois Confederacy dominated the New York and Lake Erie region.

The Europeans

The written history of what is now New York begins in 1524 when an Italian explorer, Giovanni da Verrazzano, sailed into what is now the harbor of New York City. Later he wrote: "They [a tribe of Algonquians] came toward us very cheerfully, making great sounds of admiration, showing us where we might come to land most safely with our boat." He also noted what many other new arrivals to New York City throughout the years

This illustration imagines the scene in which Peter Minuit is said to have bought the island of Manhattan for the equivalent of about $24.00.

have thought: "It seemed so commodious and delightful, and which we supposed must contain great riches."

Though Verrazzano soon sailed back to Europe, other explorers followed in search of those riches. In 1608, a Frenchman, Samuel de Champlain, set up a fur trading post near present-day Quebec, Canada. The following year, he discovered what is now known as Lake Champlain. Part of this lake lies in the northeastern section of New York State. Also, in 1609, Henry Hudson, an Englishman employed by the Dutch, sailed into what is now called New York Harbor and up the river that today bears his name. He traveled as far north as present-day Albany.

In 1624, the Dutch set up a fur trading post and settlement in what they called Fort Orange (present-day Albany). This first permanent European settlement in the region was soon followed by the settlement of New Amsterdam at the southern tip of the island of Manhattan. The New Amsterdam settlers built a wall on the northern border of the town to keep out neighboring Native Americans and English settlers. Years later, after the wall came down, the place where it had stood was named Wall Street.

By the 1660s, there were several Dutch settlements in what is now New York City. On the northern end of Manhattan was a farming community called Nieuw Haarlem (now the neighborhood known as Harlem). Across the East River was Breuckelen (now Brooklyn), and across the Harlem River a village grew around a farm owned by Jonas Bronck. The area came to be known as Bronk's Land and, later, the Bronx. All of the Dutch settlements in and around present-day New York were collectively known as New Netherland.

Before long, events in Europe intruded on the peaceful Dutch community. War broke out between England and the Netherlands, and in 1664, English warships sailed into New York Harbor. The Dutch governor, Peter Stuyvesant, seeing he was hopelessly outnumbered, surrendered New Netherland to the English. Soon afterward, King Charles II of England gave the new land to his brother, the duke of York, as a gift, and much of the former Dutch colony was renamed New York. The English allowed the Dutch settlers to remain, and soon new Dutch, French, German, and English colonists were arriving in New York.

The Native People

Long before the first settlers reached New York shores, Native people had made the region their home. The Lenape, the Algonquian, the Haudenosaunee, and other tribes lived across the state. The Lenape, also known as the Delaware, lived in the southern part of the state, where New York City is today, while the Algonquian and the Haudenosaunee, later known as the Iroquois, lived in Central and Western New York. Most tribes settled on the different waterways—the Finger Lakes, Lake Champlain, and Lake George, to name a few.

Each tribe thrived in the untamed wilderness, with unique governments, religions, and cultures. The cultures of these Native American tribes are important parts of New York's history. These tribes also had many things in common. Most got their food primarily from farming, though they also fished, hunted, and gathered. They made their houses from the bark and wood of trees—the Iroquois made long, wood houses called longhouses and the Algonquian lived in smaller, round houses known as wigwams. They also played games similar to lacrosse and told stories.

When the Europeans arrived in the New York region, they were looking for furs. They decided to trade with the Algonquain, giving them guns in exchange for fur. Guns changed the lives of the Native Americans—they could hunt more easily, and were armed with much deadlier weapons when they went to war. Guns weren't the only things Europeans introduced. Deadly diseases such as smallpox and cholera were brought over from Europe. The Native Americans did not have any resistance to these new diseases, and many of them died.

Today, there are eight federally recognized Native tribes in New York. The Seneca, Cayuga, Oneida, Onondaga, St. Regis Band of the Mohawk, Tonawanda Band of Senecas, and the Tuscarora Nations were all at one point part of the Iroquois Nation. The eighth tribe is the Shinnecock, who are located in Southhampton. Though the tribes have undergone huge changes since the Europeans settled in New York, there are still more than 100,000 Native American people who live in the state today.

Spotlight on the Iroquois Confederacy

The Iroquois Confederacy is a group of Native American tribes that lived, and continue to live, in New York State. Formed sometime between 1140 and 1600 CE, the Confederacy is one of the oldest democracies in the world.

A typical Iroquois longhouse was 180 to 220 feet (55-67 m) long.

Iroquois was a name made up by the French who first encountered the tribes in the Seventeenth Century. The Iroquois called themselves the *Haudenosaunee*, which means "People of the Longhouse."

Organizations: Iroquois villages were made up of clans. Clans were made up of families that had a common female ancestor. Each clan was named after an animal. Each tribe had chiefs who gathered together to make major decisions that affected the entire Confederacy.

Food: Iroquois women tended the vegetable fields. The three main crops that they grew were known as the Three Sisters: corn, beans, and squash. The Iroquois not only ate these vegetables, but they also used their byproducts to make cooking tools and other useful things. Iroquois men hunted deer, turkeys, rabbits, beavers, and other animals. They also fished during the spring and summer.

Women: Women held a lot of power in the Iroquois Confederacy. Women elected the chiefs and local leaders. Clan leaders were the oldest or most respected female in the family.

Fun Facts: Lacrosse's history can be traced back to games that the Iroquois played. Iroquois villages often moved every 10-20 years to find fresh land for hunting and farming.

The American Revolution and Beyond

By the mid–1700s, 13 colonies of Great Britain stretched along the Atlantic seaboard from Georgia to what is now Maine. From 1754 to 1763, the British and French battled for control of the North American fur trade. In 1763, with the help of the powerful Iroquois, the British won what came to be known as the French and Indian War. The British government had spent a great deal of money fighting the French. To raise money quickly, the British government decided to tax the American colonists. This was a fateful mistake.

Some colonists remained loyal to the British king and Parliament, but many others objected to paying for Britain's wars. These colonists felt it was unfair that they could be taxed when there was no one representing their interests thousands of

One of the colonists' earliest victories in the American Revolution was the capture of Fort Ticonderoga, overlooking Lake Champlain. The site is now open as a museum.

This picture shows British general John Burgoyne surrendering at the Battle of Saratoga, one of the most important American victories in the war for independence.

miles away in the British Parliament in London. Tensions built. "No taxation without representation!" became the cry of the day. By 1775, the colonies were at war with Britain, and the next year, they formally declared their independence. The first shots of the war were fired in Massachusetts, but New York was quickly identified as a **strategic** area. The colony lay between New England and the other colonies farther south. Britain's strategy was to occupy New York in order to split the colonies. As a result, nearly one-third of the war's battles were fought in New York. In 1776, the British occupied New York City. Not long after, in 1777, a very important battle, often called the turning point of the American Revolution, took place near Saratoga, north of Albany. After the British were defeated at the Battle of Saratoga, France decided to join the war on the American side. With French help, the colonist defeated the British and won their independence.

After the war was officially over in 1783 and the new country called the United States of America was established, a state agency called the New York Land Board bought most of the land in western New York from the Iroquois and sold it off at low prices to white settlers. Many New Englanders jumped at the chance, and soon new towns called Hudson, Ithaca, Syracuse, and Buffalo sprang up in the western and northern sections of the state.

Peace did not last for long, however. From 1812 to 1815, the United States fought

Making a Rock Ladybug

The nine-spotted ladybug has been New York's State Insect since 1989. Though no longer thought to be extinct, this species is still a very rare sight across the state. With the help of an adult, you can make your very own rock version of a ladybug. Once you are finished, you can keep it on a shelf or place it in your garden!

What You Need

Large smooth, round rock

Acrylic paint in any color

Black acrylic paint

2 wiggle eyes

Acrylic sealer spray

White glue

What to Do

- Wash and dry the rock.
- Paint the rock any color you'd like and allow it to dry. Apply a second and third coat if needed.
- Paint ¼ of one of the ends black. This will be the ladybug's head.
- Paint a straight line down the center of the rock with black paint, starting at the head and ending at the other end.
- Dip the end of a paintbrush with the black paint. Dot spots on the ladybug's back.
- Once the paint is dry, ask an adult to spray the rock with acrylic sealer spray. Allow it to dry completely.
- Using white glue, attach the wiggle eyes and let them dry.

another war with Britain, called the War of 1812. Parts of New York were turned into battlefields once more as British troops attacked Fort Niagara and destroyed neighboring farms and villages. In a second **raid**, the British burned the settlements in Buffalo. New York was also the scene of Commodore Thomas Macdonough's overwhelming victory for the American Navy in the Battle of Lake Champlain near Plattsburgh. When the war finally ended in 1815, New Yorkers were free to get back to the business of building their communities and bringing industry to all parts of the state. By 1820, almost 1.4 million people lived in New York, making it the most populated state in the country.

The Erie Canal

In the early 1800s, the people of New York realized that a canal connecting the Atlantic Ocean and the Great Lakes would create economic opportunity for New York and forge a link between the East Coast of the United States and the Midwest. DeWitt Clinton, mayor of New York City and later governor of the state, was especially enthusiastic about the idea, but most people thought it could not be done. Still, Clinton finally convinced the New York State legislature to grant $7 million for the project. Work on what was referred to as "Clinton's ditch" began in 1817. Due to the backbreaking labor of thousands of workers, the canal was ready to open eight years later.

Fifteen Miles on the Erie Canal

Mules pulled barges carrying goods along the Erie Canal. Connected to the barges by ropes, the mules walked on towpaths alongside the canal. The barges might be moved 15 miles [24 km] in a day. The song sometimes called "Fifteen Miles on the Erie Canal" talks about the job of moving freight on the canal. It begins like this:

I've got a mule, and her name is Sal,
Fifteen miles on the Erie Canal.
She's a good ol' worker and a good ol' pal,
Fifteen miles on the Erie Canal.

In the end, the canal ran 363 miles (584 km) from Albany on the Hudson River to Buffalo on the shore of Lake Erie. As hoped, the canal successfully connected the Great Lakes to the Hudson River and New York City—and helped jumpstart northwestern New York's economy. For half a century, until railroads became the major way to move freight in the 1870s, the Erie Canal was a principal route for shipping manufactured goods west and farm products east. Cities including Buffalo, Rochester, and Syracuse became much larger and wealthier during this time.

The Civil War

New York's economy was picking up, but much of the state's success was built on shaky ground—namely the institution of slavery. From the time the Dutch occupied the area, there were slaves in New York, and the practice of owning slaves in New York continued through the 1700s. Even after 1827, when slavery was abolished, or ended, in the state, some New Yorkers profited from slave labor. New York bankers and merchants lent money to and traded with cotton growers and merchants in the South. These New Yorkers made a great deal of money from the South's cotton industry, which depended on slave labor.

By the time the **American Civil War** broke out in 1861, many people in the North (including in New York State) were strongly opposed to slavery. They wanted to see it end. Not everyone was willing to fight for the cause, however.

When President Abraham Lincoln signed the Enrollment Act of 1863, a bill that established a draft into the army, many citizens were furious. With news of the bloody battle at Gettysburg on the front page of the major papers, Lincoln's call for 300,000 more soldiers frightened even those people who believed in the cause. Further, many poor people, Irish immigrants in particular, were angry that for 300 dollars wealthy citizens

This illustration shows Confederate prisoners inside Fort Lafayette, a Union-run prison in New York Harbor, during the Civil War.

Soldiers from northern New York pose for a photographer during the Civil War.

could buy their way out of service. The result was the New York City draft riots. For three days in July of 1863, mobs swarmed through the city's streets, protesting the war by looting stores and burning buildings. Union troops had to be pulled from the front lines to help restore order.

Hardship in the South

At the start of the Civil War, the value of all manufactured goods produced in all the Confederate states added up to less than one-fourth of those produced in New York State alone.

Despite the horror of the draft riots, New York State and its citizens ultimately rallied to the Union cause. In fact, by the war's end in 1865, New York State had supplied the most troops, money, arms, and food of any northern state. More than 4,000 free blacks from New York served in the Union Army. New York also suffered the greatest casualties of any state. In all, 50,000 soldiers from New York died in battle or from wounds, disease, or malnutrition.

10 KEY CITIES

New York City

Yonkers

Syracuse

1. New York City: population 8,175,133

New York City is the most populated city in the United States. The number of people who live in New York City makes up 42 percent of the entire state's population!

2. Buffalo: population 261,310

Buffalo, in Western New York, is known for its cold and snowy winters. It is where buffalo chicken wings were invented. Buffalo was also the first city in the United States to light its streets with electricity.

3. Rochester: population 210,565

Rochester has a rich music and arts culture. It is home to the Eastman School of Music, the George Eastman House International Museum of Photography and Film, and the Memorial Art Gallery.

4. Yonkers: population 195,976

Many people think Yonkers is the sixth borough of New York City because it is only a few miles (kilometers) north. Every March, Yonkers holds one of the largest St. Patrick's Day parades in the United States.

5. Syracuse: population 145,170

Nicknamed "The Salt City," Syracuse was the largest producer of salt in the United States in the 1800s. Once the Erie Canal was completed, it provided a route to ship the salt across the state and beyond, which helped Syracuse grow.

NEW YORK

6. Albany: population 97,856

Albany became New York's state capital in 1797. After the Erie Canal was built, Albany became an important port city because of its location. Goods from the Midwest could easily reach New York City and back again. Today, residents and visitors enjoy the city's entertainment venues, parks, and its proximity to major cities and mountain ranges.

7. New Rochelle: population 77,062

New Rochelle, located just northeast of New York City, was settled by the French in the late 1600s. Many of the settlers were from the French town of La Rochelle. This is how New Rochelle got its name.

8. Mount Vernon: population 67,292

Mount Vernon is a small city just north of New York City's borough, the Bronx. Mount Vernon was named after George Washington's home in Virginia.

9. Schenectady: population 66,135

Schenectady, located about 20 miles (32 km) west of Albany, is often called "The City that Lights the World." This is because the electric company General Electric is based out of the city.

10. Utica: population 62,235

After the completion of the Erie Canal, Utica became a stopping point for travelers. By the mid-1800s, Utica had grown into a small city with many businesses.

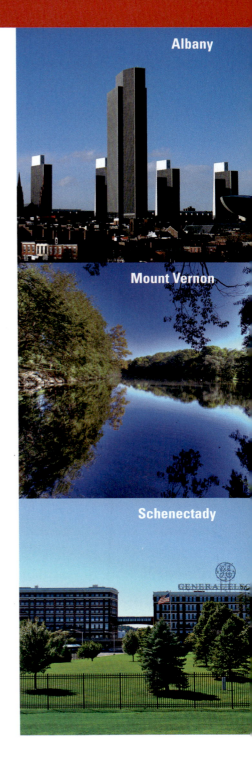

Albany

Mount Vernon

Schenectady

Industrialization

In the mid–1800s, America entered a period known as the Industrial Revolution, when new technologies and new machines made it easier for manufacturers and industries to produce goods in big factories on a large scale. Business boomed. Buffalo became the home of many steel plants. Railroad tracks were laid down throughout the state, connecting cities and towns. The first New York City elevated railway—known as the "El"—opened for business in 1870.

At the same time, a new generation of business leaders began to make its mark on American industry. In New York City, a man named Isaac Singer invented the sewing machine. Soon his factories were producing them by the hundreds. Elisha Graves Otis invented the elevator brake—an innovation that made the idea of building skyscrapers a reality. He started a company in Yonkers that made electric elevators for high-rise buildings. In Rochester, a bank teller named George Eastman invented and mass-produced the first hand-held camera, the famous "Eastman Kodak." John D. Rockefeller, who was born near Ithaca, established the Standard Oil Company and became one of the richest people in America.

The Triangle Shirtwaist Tragedy

In 1911, there was a fire at the Triangle Shirtwaist Company dress factory in New York City. The owners of the company had locked the doors so that the workers would not leave their posts during the workday. When the fire broke out, the workers were trapped, and 146 people, mostly women and children, died in the fire. This tragedy led to the creation of workplace safety laws and child labor laws.

Successful businesses needed a vibrant workforce. Technological advances in industry coincided with the first big wave of German and Irish immigrants in the mid–1800s—men and women who came to the United States in search of a better life. In the late 1800s and early 1900s, they were followed by even larger numbers of immigrants from southern and eastern Europe. Though most of these new Americans found work, it was usually in "sweatshops," factories where the owners wanted the most goods made as quickly and cheaply as possible. For most factory workers, the workday was very long, the pay was very low, and the working conditions were often unsafe and unclean. Even young children worked 12–hour days. The rich grew richer, while by 1900 huge numbers of immigrants were living

A man rides a single-man car on a New York City elevated railroad circa 1870.

in slums. New York State grew enormously in the later decades of the nineteenth century. By 1890, New York was accounting for a stunning one-sixth of the nation's manufacturing. The most important industries were men's and women's clothing, milled flour, machine-shop products, textiles, and published materials.

Early Twentieth Century

New York raced into the twentieth century with a roar. Until the end of the nineteenth century, "New York City" meant "Manhattan." In 1898, Brooklyn, the Bronx, Queens, and Staten Island officially joined New York City, increasing its area tenfold and almost doubling its population (to 3.5 million people). Now it was the second-largest city in the world, after London. Business continued to thrive. Soon the New York Stock Exchange on Wall Street was trading millions of dollars' worth of shares a day. The famous Manhattan skyline—rows of skyscrapers—began to take shape. But while industrialists built giant mansions, the slums continued to grow. New York was a state of great wealth and achievement as well as great poverty and need.

From 1919 to 1920 and again from 1923 to 1928, Al Smith was governor of New York. Among other things, Smith focused on providing better housing and welfare services for New Yorkers. He channeled money into public programs for parks, highways, and

A young New Yorker in the early 1900s carries his "homework" from a sweatshop: clothing.

bridges and instituted labor laws to protect workers—including children. Despite Smith's great achievements, there was trouble ahead for New York and America.

In 1929, the entire country was hit by the Great Depression. Many people lost their jobs. In 1931, New York governor Franklin Delano Roosevelt created the Temporary Emergency Relief Administration. New York became the first state in the nation to give state aid to the unemployed. After being elected president in 1932, Roosevelt continued where he had left off, creating what he called the New Deal, a series of nationwide public works and social-service programs designed to give aid and jobs to Americans who had been hit hardest by the Depression. Recovery was slow, but Roosevelt's policies helped New Yorkers dig themselves out of one of the most difficult periods in their history.

World War II and Beyond

In 1939, World War II began in Europe, but the United States stayed out of the fighting. However, after Japan bombed the U.S. naval base at Pearl Harbor, Hawaii, in 1941, the nation was in the war. New York State did its share in the massive effort to defeat the governments of Germany, Japan, and Italy. The Brooklyn Navy Yard became one of the largest naval shipyards in the world, and the New York port sent hundreds of convoys (fleets of ships) to the war fronts. More than 3 million troops and their equipment, as well as 63 million tons of supplies and materials, were soon shipped overseas from the Empire State. When peace came in 1945, the entire country, including New York, experienced an enormous economic boom.

Several large manufacturing companies had been established in upstate New York in the late 1800s and early 1900s. As their businesses grew, so did the need for more workers. Soon African Americans from the South and men and women from Puerto Rico poured into the state looking for work. By the 1960s, the racial tension and civil unrest that could be felt around the country bubbled over in New York. On July 18, 1964, riots erupted in Harlem. Less than a week later, on July 24, there were riots in Rochester. The state's National Guard had to be called in to restore order. This was the first time the National Guard had ever been called in to a northern city.

Did You Know?

Zippers became widely used during the Great Depression because buttons were too expensive.

New York governor Nelson Rockefeller responded to the problems facing many **minorities** by setting aside funds for housing and job training for the poor. Though Rockefeller's policies were meant to help people and sometimes did, their cost strained the state government's budget. In the 1970s, the governments of both New York State and New York City faced serious financial problems.

These New Yorkers, out of work and out of money, stand in a "breadline," waiting to receive free food during the Great Depression.

Times Square, in New York City, is often called "The Crossroads of the World." It is a popular tourist destination and the center of the theater district.

New York Today

After narrowly steering clear of financial **disaster**, New York quickly rebounded. Good economic times nationwide for most of the 1980s and 1990s helped New Yorkers. As New York's economy shifted from manufacturing to service industries, such as banking, people all over the state benefited. Between 1980 and 1990, more than one million new jobs were created across New York. New York City, in particular, benefited from the economic boom in the banking and finance industry. Young professionals increasingly saw the city as a desirable place to live and work. Rudolph Giuliani, New York's mayor from 1994 until 2001, also worked to improve the city's image. For years crime was rampant in Manhattan and other parts of the city, and many areas, such as Times Square, were considered seedy and dangerous. Mayor Giuliani focused on adding more police to the streets and bringing the city's crime problem

In Their Own Words

"The city [Manhattan] seen from the Queensboro Bridge is always the city seen for the first time, in its first wild promise of all the mystery and beauty in the world."
–F. Scott Fitzgerald, American novelist

Graffiti was a big problem in New York City during the 1980s. Mayor Giuliani focused on cleaning it up as a way to improve the city's image.

under control. (In the early twenty-first century, New York City had one of the lowest crime rates of any major city in America.) Giuliani also cleaned up Times Square, making it more family—and tourist—friendly. By the mid–1990s, New York City came to be admired as an exciting place, home to creative, interesting people. Indeed, there was a new shine on the Big Apple.

The Brooklyn Bridge

Shortly before Brooklyn became part of New York City, the first bridge connecting Manhattan and Brooklyn was completed. The Brooklyn Bridge opened in 1883. The world's longest suspension bridge at the time, it was considered a great engineering achievement, and it is still considered one of the most beautiful bridges ever constructed. In 1964, the National Park Service named the Brooklyn Bridge a National Historic Landmark.

Then, on the morning of September 11, 2001, tragedy struck. Terrorists hijacked four airplanes. At 8:46 a.m., the terrorists crashed one of the planes into the top floors of the North Tower of Manhattan's famous World Trade Center's Twin Towers. At about 9:02 a.m. a second plane crashed into the South Tower. Though some people managed to escape from the burning buildings, many were not so lucky. By the end of the day, both enormous towers had collapsed, and almost 3,000 people were dead. Among them were 60 police officers and 343 firefighters. A third plane was flown into the Pentagon (the U.S. Department of Defense headquarters, outside Washington, D.C.). The fourth plane crashed in a field near Pittsburgh, Pennsylvania. The September 11 terrorist attack was the worst such attack ever to occur on American soil.

The destruction of the World Trade Center's Twin Towers was a national tragedy that was particularly **devastating** for New York City. But out of disaster, New Yorkers bonded as never before and showed the world the unique nature of their strength and spirit. Volunteers rushed downtown to search for survivors and to help clear debris. Others lined up to donate blood and feed the firefighters and other rescue workers who were working at the site. Money poured in to aid families of victims. The incredible bravery of the firefighters and police officers was acknowledged worldwide, as was Mayor Giuliani's skillful leadership during the city's darkest days.

Over time, the citizens of New York got back to business as usual. A 1,776-foot (541-m) tall skyscraper now stands next to the site of the former World Trade Center's Twin Towers. The site also includes a memorial to the victims and a museum.

10 KEY DATES IN STATE HISTORY

1. 300CE

Mound Builders from the Mississippi and Ohio river valleys inhabit what is now New York.

2. April 17, 1524

Giovanni da Verrazzano becomes the first European to sail into what is now called New York Harbor. Today, a bridge in New York City is named after him, however the bridge is spelled with only one "z."

3. September, 1609

Henry Hudson sails as far as present-day Albany, New York, up the river that now bears his name. His ship is called the *Half Moon*. Along the way, he traded with local Native American tribes.

4. August, 1664

The British take control of Dutch New Netherland after Governor Peter Stuyvesant surrenders. Much of the city is renamed New York.

5. July 26, 1788

New York ratifies the new U.S. Constitution and officially enters the Union as the eleventh state.

6. October 26, 1825

After eight years of construction, the Erie Canal is completed. It was enlarged between 1836 and 1862.

7. October 29, 1929

The stock-market crash marks the beginning of the Great Depression and one of the toughest decades in New York and American history. The day is often called "Black Tuesday."

8. September 11, 2001

Terrorists hijack four planes, crashing two of them into New York City's World Trade Center. The other two planes crashed into the Pentagon in Washington, D.C. and a field in Shanksville, Pennsylvania.

9. January, 2009

New York Senator Hillary Clinton becomes U.S. Secretary of State.

10. October 29, 2012

Hurricane Sandy hits New York City. It was the second-costliest hurricane in U.S. history, and more than 100 people in the U.S. died.

The Statue of Liberty, in New York Harbor, was a welcome site to immigrants who spent an average of 7 to 21 days aboard a ship crossing the Atlantic Ocean.

The People

For a century or more, beginning in the mid–1800s, New York City served as the main entry point for immigrants into the United States. It continues to be a major point of entry today. As a result, New York has become one of the most ethnically diverse states in the nation. As New York journalist Daniel J. Wakin said, "It's the unique mix of people that keeps New York State vibrant and strong." Although the United States is often called the great American melting pot, it is probably more accurate to think of it as a giant tossed salad. People who come to America hold onto aspects of their culture and traditions even as they blend into American society. New York represents the same tossed salad on a smaller scale.

The immigrants of the mid–1800s came mostly from Germany and Ireland. Escaping poverty and **famine**, these men and women came in such large numbers that by 1850 half the people living in New York City were foreign born. In the 1880s, the city's population doubled when a new wave of immigration began. People from Italy, other southern European countries, and eastern Europe began coming to America in large numbers, escaping poverty and religious **persecution** and looking for economic opportunity and greater freedom. That wave of immigration continued through the early decades of the twentieth century.

Lady Liberty

The Statue of Liberty was a gift from the people of France to the people of America. It represented the friendship between the two countries that was established during the American Revolution, as well as the ideals behind that war: liberty and the pursuit of happiness. The statue was built in France, shipped to the United States in pieces in 214 crates, and then assembled on an island in New York Harbor. Dedicated in 1886, Lady Liberty began welcoming the millions of immigrants entering the harbor—and the United States—by ship in the following decades.

For more than four decades starting in 1924, the U.S. government strictly limited the number of immigrants admitted to the United States. After these **restrictions** were eased in the late 1960s, New York again became the destination of choice for many immigrants. Since 1980, for example, more than 400,000 Russian Jews have moved to the Big Apple. But many of the new immigrants have come from places other than Europe, including Asia, Africa, the Caribbean, Central America, and Mexico. New York City is home to people of practically every religion and nationality in the world.

If you are in New York City and in the mood for Chinese food, just take a downtown train to Manhattan's Chinatown. Feel like a cannoli afterward for dessert? Stroll just a few blocks to Little Italy. Indian food? No problem. Any native New Yorker will tell you: Head to Sixth Street between First and Second Avenues in Manhattan. You will find dozens of Indian restaurants lining the street. Or take the train uptown to Harlem, home of some of the best barbecue and old-style southern-cooking restaurants in the country. Of course, you do not have to go to a specific area of town to sample different cultures. There are Chinese, Thai, Indian, Korean, Japanese, Vietnamese, Mexican, and Italian restaurants and groceries all over New York City—most likely within a five-minute walk of wherever you might be. There are synagogues and churches and mosques throughout the city too, as well as places of worship for followers of many other religions.

The Big Apple

There is a reason why many of the people who come to the United States decide to make New York City their home. As the home to so many businesses and industries, the city

Ellis Island was the first stop for immigrants coming to America for the first time.

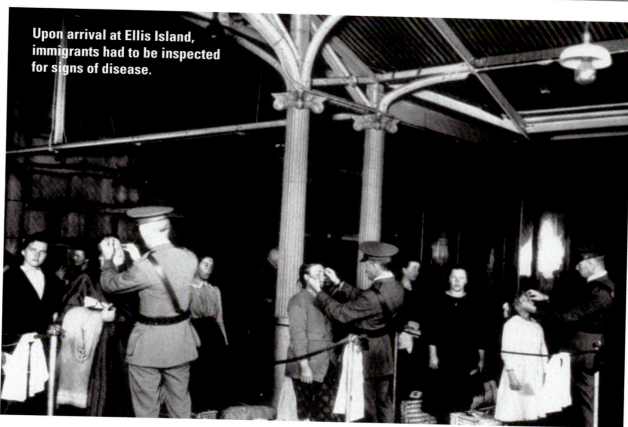

Upon arrival at Ellis Island, immigrants had to be inspected for signs of disease.

10 KEY PEOPLE

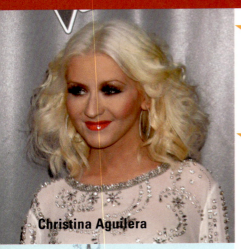

Christina Aguilera

Jay-Z

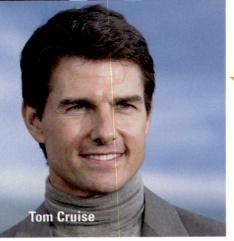

Tom Cruise

1. Christina Aguilera

Christina Aguilera is a singer, songwriter, and a judge on the TV show *The Voice*. She was born in Staten Island, New York, which is one of New York City's five boroughs.

2. L. Frank Baum

L. Frank Baum is the author of one of the most loved books of all time, *The Wonderful Wizard of Oz*. Every spring his hometown of Chittenango holds a festival, called the Oz-Stravaganza, to celebrate the story.

3. Shawn Carter [Jay-Z]

The artist rose to fame in the mid–1990s by writing about his experiences growing up in the tough Marcy Projects public housing development. By 2007, Jay-Z had tied Elvis Presley's record for most number-one albums by a solo performer.

4. Tom Cruise

Tom Cruise is one of the biggest movie stars in the world. Born in Syracuse, Tom's real name is Thomas Cruise Mapother IV. He has been in some of the most successful movies of all time, including the *Mission Impossible* series, *War of the Worlds*, and *Jerry Maguire*.

5. Ruth Bader Ginsberg

Ruth Bader Ginsberg is an Associate Justice of the U.S. Supreme Court. She is only the second woman and the first Jewish woman to hold this position. Ginsberg was born and raised in Brooklyn in New York City, where she went to school and worked in a garment factory.

NEW YORK

6. Michael Jordan

Michael Jordan is often called one of the greatest basketball players of all time. He helped the Chicago Bulls win six NBA Championships. Jordan is known for his athletic ability and star power. Before moving to North Carolina, he lived in Brooklyn.

7. Tom Kenny

Tom Kenny is a comedian, actor, and the voice of the cartoon character SpongeBob SquarePants. He is from East Syracuse, New York, where he went to school and was also the lead singer of a band called The Tearjerkers.

8. Jennifer Lopez

Jennifer Lopez is a singer, dancer, and actress from the Bronx, New York. Growing up in a tough neighborhood, Lopez stayed busy by running track and taking dance classes. In 2012, *Forbes* magazine named her the most powerful celebrity in the world.

9. Norman Rockwell

Born in 1894 in New York City, Rockwell always knew he wanted to be an artist, and he started getting jobs as early as his teens. Rockwell became known for his depiction of normal, everyday American life. His most famous works are his covers for *The Saturday Evening Post* magazine.

10. Elizabeth Cady Stanton

Elizabeth Cady Stanton, an activist from Johnstown, presented a document called the "Declaration of Sentiments" at the first women's rights **convention** in Seneca Falls, New York, in 1848. Stanton's declaration is often referred to as the beginning of the women's rights movement in the U.S.

Michael Jordan

Jennifer Lopez

Norman Rockwell

Who New Yorkers Are

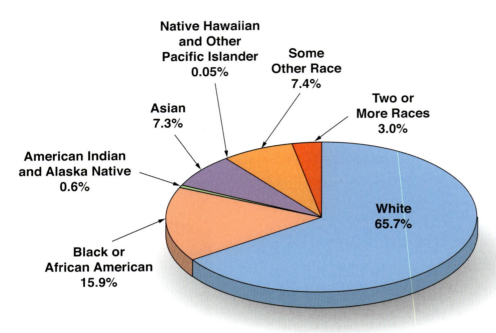

Native Hawaiian and Other Pacific Islander 0.05%

Some Other Race 7.4%

Asian 7.3%

Two or More Races 3.0%

American Indian and Alaska Native 0.6%

White 65.7%

Black or African American 15.9%

Total Population
19,378,102

Hispanic or Latino (of any race):
• 3,416,922 people (17.6%)

Note: The pie chart shows the racial breakdown of the state's population based on the categories used by the U.S. Bureau of the Census. The Census Bureau reports information for Hispanics or Latinos separately, since they may be of any race. Percentages in the pie chart may not add to 100 because of rounding.

Source: U.S. Bureau of the Census, 2010 Census

offers a wide range of job opportunities. The city is also one of the leading cultural centers of the nation and indeed the world. Manhattan offers some of the world's finest museums, internationally renowned theater, and world-class music and dance.

In Their Own Words

"I look out the window and I see the lights and the skyline and the people on the street rushing around looking for action, love, and the world's greatest chocolate chip cookie, and my heart does a little dance."
—Nora Ephron, writer

As Madeleine Hyde, a native New Yorker and teacher, put it: "Come to New York. Whatever you want, we've got it."

Some people come to New York to enjoy these entertainments. Others—artists, such as actors, dancers, musicians, and more—come hoping to make their big break into show business. As Frank Sinatra famously sang about New York: "If I can make it there, I'll make it anywhere."

Something for Everyone

New York's cultural attractions are not limited to New York City. A state as big and diverse as New York has much to offer. Since 1863, historic Saratoga Springs, near Albany, has been home to a famous horseracing track. Saratoga is also where you will find the Saratoga Performing Arts Center—the summer residence for the New York City Opera, the New York City Ballet, and the Philadelphia Orchestra. Art lovers are sure to appreciate the Hyde Collection, which can be found in Glens Falls. This museum includes works by some of the finest European and American artists. The Bethel Woods Center for the Arts is located on the site of the famous 1969 Woodstock music festival. Today, visitors come to enjoy concerts in every musical genre, from classical to pop. The quiet village of Cooperstown is home to the National Baseball Hall of Fame and Museum, as well as several other museums and historic homes.

In upstate New York, there are simple pleasures around every corner. The people of Buffalo are proud of the beautiful old stone houses with large porches that line their city streets, not to mention the five homes designed by world-famous architect Frank Lloyd Wright. Nearby, the majestic waterfalls of Niagara Falls remain a major tourist attraction.

Central Park is a popular place for New Yorkers to relax and enjoy the outdoors.

In Rochester, home to Xerox and Eastman Kodak, the citizens are pleased with their city's nickname: the image capital. Many citizens enjoy taking walks along the Erie Canal at night. Residents are also proud of the city's history of social consciousness. Susan B. Anthony, who fought for women's voting rights, lived in Rochester. And Frederick Douglass, the African-American leader of the movement to end slavery, is buried in the city where he lived and where he gave many of his most rousing speeches.

Syracuse is home to the Great New York State Fair, a 12–day-long fair that marks the end of summer. Basketball lovers enjoy going to the Carrier Dome to root for the Syracuse Orange, Syracuse University's Division I basketball team. On February 1, 2014, visitors broke the Dome's attendance record when 35,446 people came to watch the Orange play their rivals, the Duke Blue Devils.

The Albany area is home to the New York State Museum and several entertainment venues, including the Palace Theatre, The Egg, Times Union Center, and Proctor's Theatre in Schenectady. Albany also hosts many festivals throughout the year, such as the Tulip Festival, PearlPalooza, and LarkFEST.

Residents and visitors alike enjoy watching New York's many professional sports teams. Basketball fans can see the Knicks (National Basketball Association) or the Liberty (Women's National Basketball Association) play at New York City's Madison Square Garden. New York has three National Hockey League teams: the Buffalo Sabres, New York Islanders, and New York Rangers. It also has three National Football League teams—the Buffalo Bills, New York Giants, and New York Jets—though the last two actually play their home games across the Hudson River in New Jersey. Both of New York's Major League Baseball teams got new stadiums in 2009. The New York Mets play at Citi Field in Queens. In their first year in a new Yankee Stadium in the Bronx, the New York Yankees won their 27th World Series in 2009, continuing their tradition as the most successful team in the history of Major League Baseball.

Largest City

In terms of population, New York City is by far the largest city in the United States. In 2010, almost 8.2 million people lived in New York City. That was more than twice the number of people living in Los Angeles, the country's second-largest city.

"My office is at Yankee Stadium. Yes, dreams do come true."—Derek Jeter, shortstop, New York Yankees

Derek Jeter has been playing Major League Baseball for the Yankees since 1995.

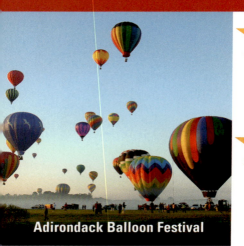

Adirondack Balloon Festival

Great NY State Fair

Harborfest

1. Adirondack Balloon Festival in Glens Falls

The festival features five balloon launches over four days with more than 350 hot air balloons of all shapes and sizes. There are also activities for children, art shows, and fireworks.

2. Canal Fest of the Tonawandas

This eight-day festival, held in North Tonawanda every July in honor of the Erie Canal, features fishing contests, rubber-duck races, chain–saw carving, and concerts by the Buffalo Philharmonic Orchestra.

3. Empire State Winter Games in Lake Placid

Every year in February, Lake Placid holds the Winter Games for amateur athletes across the state. Events include figure skating, skiing, and bobsledding. Lake Placid was the home of the Olympic Winter Games in 1932 and 1980.

4. Great New York State Fair in Syracuse

Held during the last few weeks of August through Labor Day, this fair includes rides, exhibits, food, and concerts. It is one of the oldest state fairs in the United States. More than 800,000 people attend the New York State Fair each year.

5. Harborfest in Oswego

More than 250,000 people a year attend this summer festival on Lake Ontario, near the town of Oswego. The festival includes concerts, food, and vendors. Harborfest, though, is best known for its huge fireworks show on Saturday night. It is considered to be one of the best fireworks displays in Upstate New York.

NEW YORK ★ ★ ★ ★

6. Macy's Thanksgiving Day Parade

Since 1924, Macy's has put on a Thanksgiving Day parade in Manhattan, featuring floats and huge balloons. Each year, more than 3 million people line the streets of New York City to watch the parade. In addition to floats and balloons, there are also marching bands, dancers, and famous singers.

7. Racing Season in Saratoga Springs

From July through September, the oldest racetrack in the U.S. holds thoroughbred horse racing. People from all parts of the state travel to watch the races. The highlight of the racing season is the Travers Stakes, which thousands of people attend each year.

8. Renaissance Festival in Sterling

A re-creation of a typical English festival in the Renaissance, featuring actors dressed in period costumes, is held on weekends from early July through mid-August. There are a lot of fun activities for kids.

9. Rochester International Jazz Festival

More than 180,000 visitors attend this festival each year. Over nine days, more than 250 concerts are held throughout the city. Some of the country's most popular jazz artists have played the festival.

10. Tulip Festival in Albany

Held every spring, this festival celebrates the area's Dutch heritage with more than 200,000 tulips, music, art, and food. There is also the naming of a Tulip Queen and a Tulip Ball.

Macy's Thanksgiving Day Parade

Rochester Jazz Festival

Tulip Festival

How the Government Works

New York State's government is headquartered in Albany, the state capital. This is where the state legislature meets and where the executive mansion, the governor's official residence, is located. In 2010, New York was represented in the U.S. Congress in Washington, D.C., by two senators and twenty-nine members in the House of Representatives.

How New York Votes

Both of America's major political parties—the Democratic Party and the Republican Party—are well represented in New York State's government. On Election Day, Republican candidates tend to do better upstate, while Democratic candidates tend to do better in and around New York City. Overall, the state had 11.8 million registered voters in 2013. More than 5.8 million of them had registered as supporters of the Democratic Party, and more than half of those voters lived in New York City. Of the 2.8 million voters who had registered as supporters of the Republican Party, less than 18 percent lived in New York City.

One of the challenges of governing a state like New York is balancing the needs and preferences of the residents of its cities with those in rural communities. "Drive through a town like Whitehall," says John Buck, longtime New York resident. "It's small and rural—

almost like Vermont. Sometimes it's hard to believe that we vote for the same governor as the people in the big city."

Branches of Government

Executive

The chief executive officer of the state, New York's governor is elected to a four-year term and is responsible for enforcing the state's laws, appointing judges, drawing up the state government's budget, and introducing legislation that might be enacted into law.

Legislative

As in most other states (and the federal government), New York's legislature is divided into two houses: the senate with 62 members and the assembly with 150 members, all elected to two-year terms. The legislature passes the state's laws and approves the government's budget. Legislators can pass a law by a simple majority vote in both houses. If the governor vetoes a measure passed by the legislature, a two-thirds vote in both houses is needed to override the veto and enact the law.

Judicial

New York's highest court, the court of appeals, is made up of a chief justice and six associate justices, all appointed to fourteen-year terms. They hear cases appealed from lower courts. The next-highest level of courts is the appellate division of the supreme court, which mostly hears appeals from lower courts. Its justices are appointed by the governor. New York calls the court below this the supreme court. Its justices are elected to fourteen-year terms. Most cases start in the supreme court.

How a Bill Becomes a Law

As in any government, the senators and members of the assembly in Albany have to work together to pass new legislation and deal with statewide problems. Though Republicans and Democrats often disagree about the correct way to attack a problem, they are ultimately faced with a choice: compromise or get nothing done. And New York government is often all about compromise. Until 2009, Republicans had a majority in the state senate for almost 40 years. On the other hand, the assembly had been under Democratic control since 1974. The leaders of these two houses, the senate majority leader and the speaker of the assembly, wield enormous power. Not only do these two people decide what is voted on in their houses, they often negotiate directly with the governor. This way of operating has caused some critics to refer to New York government as three people in a room. Though the senate

This is the Senate Chamber inside the New York State Capitol, in Albany.

majority leader and the speaker of the assembly always need the votes of their members in the legislature to pass a bill, their influence is so enormous that when they and the governor agree to do something, it is almost certain to happen.

Of course, not all the power lies with the leaders of the two houses and the governor.

Most new bills start with a single senator or assembly member who introduces his or her idea to one chamber of the legislature. Once a bill is introduced, it is referred to a standing committee for debate. At this point the bill can be rejected. But if a majority of committee members support the new bill, the full senate or assembly can debate and vote on it. If the bill gets a majority vote, it is passed to the other legislative house, which will then debate it. But even if the bill is approved in the other house, its journey to becoming a law is not over yet. The senate and the assembly often pass different versions. These need to be ironed out in a committee. When the senate and the assembly finally agree on the details and wording of the bill, they send it to the governor for signature. If the governor signs it, it becomes a law. If the governor does not like the bill, he or she can veto (or reject) it. Both houses of the legislature then must pass the bill again by a two-thirds vote to override a veto and make the bill a law. If they do not, then the bill dies.

Education

New York is home to a variety of public and private schools. From kindergarten and elementary school all the way to college, the state provides many opportunities for learning. However, quality education—whether public or private—requires money for teachers, supplies, and other resources students need. Funding for education is a major issue for state voters and legislators. About 3 million students attend public schools in New York State, and a major concern of many New Yorkers is the quality of public education. According to New York senator Eric Schneiderman, "The biggest problem facing New York State is how to fix the public education system. A substantial number of kids are nowhere near reading level. If you don't have a trained workforce, you can't compete in the global economy."

For years, many New Yorkers complained that public schools were not getting enough funding from the state. Others saw problems not so much with the total amount of

One of the state's most famous schools, the U.S. Military Academy, is located at West Point, New York. The school relies mostly on military and government funding.

state funding as with the way that funding was distributed. Early in 2001, a New York supreme court justice, Leland DeGrasse, ruled that the state's formula for dividing up money among different school districts was racially biased. Judge DeGrasse ruled that the state had to come up with ways to give more money to New York City schools, many of which have large African-American, Hispanic, and Asian-American student bodies. Then-Governor George Pataki fought the ruling for years. On the other side, in favor of more funding for city schools, was an organization called the Campaign for Fiscal Equity. Eventually, in 2007 after a new governor had taken office, state funding for New York City schools was increased.

America's Favorite Uncle

The man who invented the character of Uncle Sam to represent the United States was from Troy, New York, near Albany. During the War of 1812, Sam Wilson, a meatpacker, stamped "U.S. Beef" on barrels of his products. When soldiers asked him what U.S. stood for, Wilson jokingly replied, "Uncle Sam." The name stuck, and the image gained fame—especially after U.S. Army posters featuring Uncle Sam and the slogan "I Want You" were printed and posted as the country geared up for World War I.

Some New Yorkers, mostly residents of wealthy communities, have a different complaint. They feel that the state's requirement that students pass a series of exams before heading on to high school should apply only to school districts that are doing poorly.

In 2009, though, the most important concern became the amount of money available for public education. The whole U.S. economy was in a severe recession. Because of the hard economic times, governments in New York, like those almost everywhere else in the country, had less money to spend and had to make cuts in funding for public schools.

Also affected by the budget crisis was the State University of New York (SUNY). With almost 450,000 students and 64 campuses, SUNY is one of the largest state university systems in the country. After state funding for SUNY was reduced, the university raised the tuition that it charges students.

Recently, parents and teachers across the state began voicing their concern over the Common Core, a set of standards that detail what students are supposed to know in English and math at the end of each grade. Many parents and teachers feel that Common Core includes too many tests, that the teaching pace is too fast, and that it hurts children who need extra help in school.

⭐ Shirley Chisholm, U.S. Congress, 1968-1982

Shirley Chisholm was born in Brooklyn in 1924. In 1968, she became the first African-American woman elected to Congress. In 1972, Chisholm became the first black woman to mount a serious campaign for the Democratic Party's nomination for president.

⭐ Rudolph "Rudy" Giuliani Mayor of New York City, 1994-2001

Rudy Giuliani was born in Brooklyn, New York in 1944. In 1994, Giuliani began his first of two terms as mayor of New York City. He is often credited as the mayor who helped reduce crime in the city, improved the quality of life for New Yorkers and tourists, and made it safer and more attractive.

⭐ Franklin D. Roosevelt, U.S. President, 1933-1945

Franklin D. Roosevelt was born in 1882 in Hyde Park, New York. President of the United States from 1933 until his death in 1945, Roosevelt helped steer the country through the Great Depression and World War II.

NEW YORK
YOU CAN MAKE A DIFFERENCE

What You Can Do

In a state as large as New York, people sometimes feel that they have no power to affect their government. In fact that is not true. "There are lots of ways to get involved," says Senator Schneiderman. "You can work for a community agency. Or contact your elected officials. If I get a hundred phone calls about a certain issue, that issue is high up on my radar screen."

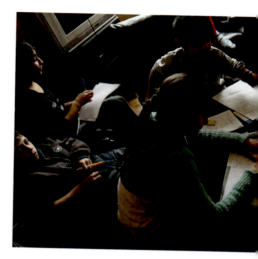

Young people can make a difference. In 1998, the deputy campaign manager for Eric Schneiderman's senate bid was David Gringer, an eleventh grader at Stuyvesant High School in New York City. His assistant was Micah Lasher—a tenth grader!

"Campaigns are always looking for people to help out," a New York community board member said. "Just show up and start stuffing envelopes."

Of course, even people who are not interested in full-time involvement can keep up-to-date by reading one of New York's many newspapers, either in print or online. Or they can form a political club to learn about and discuss issues of the day and to let elected officials know how they feel about these issues.

Contacting Lawmakers

There are two websites that can help people contact members of the state legislature.

To contact a member of the New York State Senate, go to:

www.nysenate.gov/contact_form

Under "Find My Senator," put in your address and zip code and click "Submit."

To find an email address for a member of the New York State Assembly, visit:

assembly.state.ny.us

Select "Assembly Members" and then select the person to whom you want to write.

The New York Stock Exchange, in New York City, is a symbol of New York State's economy.

Making a Living

New York State has enjoyed a history of great economic success, which today is supported by a workforce of more than 8 million people. Just as New York is home to people of many different backgrounds, it is also home to a wide variety of industries—from farming to fashion to finance. Some industries are tied to specific regions. Others can be found throughout the state.

The Road to Progress

Much of the state's early success can be traced to its key role in transportation and shipping. New York Harbor is one of the best natural harbors on the Atlantic coast—a sheltered harbor that large ships can enter. Even in the early 1800s, New York City was a major port. Then, the opening of the Erie Canal in 1825 created a water route connecting the city and its port with western New York and the Midwest. With later expansions, the current 524-mile (843-km) New York State Canal System links the Great Lakes to the Hudson River and five waterways in Canada. The trade route created by the canal system touches almost every major city in New York.

Today, New York is also crisscrossed by miles and miles of highways for moving products—and people—across the state. The Governor Thomas E. Dewey Thruway links

New York City and Buffalo. It also has extensions that connect it to major highways in Massachusetts, Pennsylvania, New Jersey, and Connecticut. The 641-mile (1,032-km) Thruway system is the longest toll-supported highway system in the United States.

The state also has thousands of miles of commercial and passenger railroad tracks. The commercial lines carry freight. Passenger lines serving New York include Amtrak and two large commuter lines in the New York City area: Metro North Railroad and the Long Island Rail Road.

Millions of people get to and from their jobs in and around New York City each day by using one of the commuter railroads or the New York City subway system. The Long Island Rail Road, which is made up of more than 700 miles (1,125 km) of track, is the busiest commuter railroad in the United States. It runs from the eastern tip of Long Island, through suburban Suffolk and Nassau counties, and into Queens, Brooklyn, and Manhattan. Metro North, which connects New York City with its northern suburbs in Westchester and other counties and with northeastern suburbs in Connecticut, is the second-busiest commuter line. This system is composed of 775 miles (1,245 km) of track. The New York City subway system is the country's largest and busiest urban mass transit system.

In addition to providing transportation, these railroad systems provide jobs. Tens of thousands of New Yorkers work for the railroads and subway system. Thousands of others work at New York's airports.

The transportation industry also includes trucking, bus and taxi service, and water transportation. New York State is home to five major seaports. The Port of Albany is located on the Hudson River, where it connects to the New York State Canal System. From there, cargo—including everything from grain to giant segments of pipe for pipelines—can be carried by truck, rail, or air to its final destination. The Port of Buffalo is located at the eastern end of Lake Erie. It is the first major port of call for foreign goods entering the United States via the Great Lakes. The Ogdensburg Port is the northernmost port in New York and is the only U.S. port on the Saint Lawrence Seaway. The Port of Oswego is located on Lake Ontario. The Port of New York and New Jersey, located in New York

Harbor, is the largest port complex on the East Coast. In 2010, the port handled more than $175 billion worth of cargo.

The Business of New York

Before 1950, manufacturing industries employed one-third of the state's workers. By the early twenty-first century, however, fewer than one in ten New Yorkers in the workforce was working in manufacturing. Although no longer the backbone of the New York economy, manufacturing still plays an important part. It is especially strong in certain areas of the state. Rochester, for example, is home to more than 1,400 manufacturing companies. Among other goods, they produce photographic and copier equipment and scientific instruments. Factories in Syracuse make paper products, telecommunications equipment, construction materials, and more.

As manufacturing declined, other parts of the state's economy grew. Today, one out of every four New York workers is employed in education or health care. This sector of the economy includes teachers, doctors, nurses, health-care technicians, therapists, and social workers. Many New Yorkers are also employed in retail trade. They sell everything from groceries to clothes to automobiles. These types of jobs can be found throughout the state.

New York City has 722 miles (1,162 km) of subway track. More than 5.3 million people ride the subway every day.

10 KEY INDUSTRIES

Construction

Agriculture

Healthcare

1. Construction

Construction workers are responsible for building everything from small homes to the tallest skyscrapers in New York City. Without them, there would be no homes and businesses.

2. Agriculture

New York is a leading fruit and vegetable producer. Vegetable farms produce cabbage, peas, corn, and tomatoes. The state's leading fruit crops are apples and grapes. Field crops include hay and field corn, which are used to feed New York's livestock.

3. Entertainment

New York City is the entertainment capital of the East Coast. Movies, TV shows, plays, musicals, and concerts employ actors and musicians. They also employ many people behind the scenes. At any given time, there are TV shows or movies being filmed somewhere in New York City!

4. Healthcare

There are more than 19 million people in New York State, many of whom need medical care from time to time. Doctors, nurses, and home-health aides are just some of the many people who take care of them.

5. Hospitality and Food Service

There are so many great places to visit in New York. Those who do visit need to eat and rest. Restaurants and hotels are big business in the Empire State, especially around the state's biggest tourist attraction, New York City.

NEW YORK

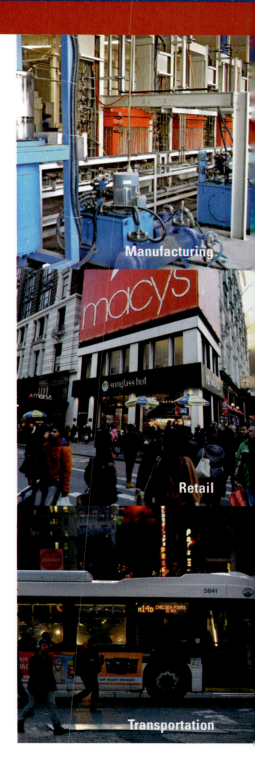
Manufacturing
Retail
Transportation

6. Publishing

New York City is considered the publishing capital of the world. Four of the United States' largest newspapers are based there (*The New York Times*, *The Wall Street Journal*, *Daily News*, and *New York Post*). Major magazine and book publishers are located there as well.

7. Manufacturing

Manufacturing is a large industry in New York, and New Yorkers are proud of the products that are made there. Some of them include Corning glass, pharmaceuticals, machinery, and computer chips.

8. Dairy Farming

Out of the 1.4 million cattle in New York, around 625,000 cows are used for dairy farming. Milk is the primary agricultural product made in the state. More than 700 million pounds (318 million kg) of cheese is produced in New York, making it the fourth largest cheese-producing state in the country.

9. Retail

The retail business is one of the largest in the state. Whether in a mall or a big city, New Yorkers and the state's visitors love to shop! No matter what kind of store it is, cashiers and salespeople must keep the store running smoothly and the customers happy.

10. Transportation

Bus drivers, subway and train workers, and truck drivers are just some of the people working in the transportation field. They help keep New York moving!

Recipe for Apple Turnovers

Apple picking is a popular activity to do in the fall in New York. Whether you pick them yourself or buy them at the store, you can use your apples to make apple turnovers. Just ask an adult to help you and follow this recipe.

What You Need

2 sheets frozen puff pastry

2 Granny Smith apples

1 tablespoon (15 ml) lemon juice

½ teaspoon (2.5 g) ground cinnamon

1 tablespoon (14.7 g) flour

1 tablespoon (14.7 g) sugar

2 tablespoons (29.4 g) brown sugar

1 egg

1 teaspoon (5 g) butter

What to Do

- Preheat oven to 350°F (180°C).
- Thaw pastry sheets on the kitchen counter for 10 minutes.
- Ask an adult to help you peel the apples and remove their cores. Slice them into small 1-inch pieces.
- Toss sliced apples with lemon juice, cinnamon, flour, and both sugars. Set aside.
- Slice each sheet of pastry into quarters.
- Spoon 1 tablespoon of the apple mixture into the center of each square, leaving room around the edges.
- Fold the square over into a triangle, and press the edges together.
- Butter a baking sheet and beat the egg.
- Brush turnovers with the egg.
- Place a few slashes in the top of the turnover so it releases steam.
- Bake for 15 minutes until golden brown.
- Eat by itself or with vanilla ice cream.

Certain industries are concentrated mainly in New York City. In fact, the city is known the world over as a leading center of banking and finance, publishing, fashion, and entertainment.

The New York Stock Exchange (NYSE) is located in the heart of New York's financial district, the Wall Street area at the southern end of Manhattan. There, brokers trade stocks and bonds. (Stocks are shares in the ownership of a corporation.) The NYSE is the largest stock exchange in the world. The New York Mercantile Exchange is also located in the Wall Street area. This is the world's largest physical **commodities** exchange. Physical commodities are agricultural products, such as corn and wheat, as well as minerals, such as gold. Brokers at the Mercantile Exchange also trade in commodities such as gasoline and heating oil. Large brokerage houses, insurance companies, and the world's leading financial institutions can all be found in New York City.

The fashion industry employs almost 100,000 people in New York State, and Manhattan is the heart of the industry. Not only is New York one of the fashion centers that sets the style for the world, it is home to such designers as Ralph Lauren, Kenneth Cole, and Tommy Hilfiger. The city also hosts the U.S. offices of foreign fashion firms, such as Prada and Chanel.

New York City is also a world leader in communications and entertainment. Many of the biggest media companies in the world, including Disney/ABC, Time Warner, and the Hearst Corporation, have their headquarters there. Hundreds of newspapers, including the *New York Times* and *Wall Street Journal*, are published in New York, as are countless books and magazines. Many movies, TV shows, and even commercials are shot in New York City, creating jobs for New Yorkers and adding money to the state's economy.

New York City is considered by many to be a cultural capital of the world. Tourism and entertainment contribute a **significant** amount to the state's economy. More than 52 million people visited New York City in 2012, making it the country's top tourist destination. They flock to Manhattan to see a Broadway play, attend an opera at the Metropolitan Opera House, or listen to the New York Philharmonic at Avery Fisher Hall.

Many also come to visit New York's many fine museums, including the Metropolitan Museum of Art, the Museum of Modern Art, the American Museum of Natural History, and the Guggenheim.

Tourism is not limited to the city, however. In 2012, there were 202 million visitors to New York State. The Greater Niagara area boasts a world-class **symphony**, wonderful art collections, and, of course, the falls. The Catskill Mountains offer skiing, rock climbing, and hiking. The Hudson Valley region is home to many historic homes and mansions, including Franklin D. Roosevelt's home and the Vanderbilt Mansion in Hyde Park. The Hudson Valley is also a great place to experience the Northeast's famous fall foliage. North of the Hudson Valley, Lake George and Lake Champlain offer visitors the opportunity to enjoy boating and water sports in spectacularly beautiful surroundings.

Orchards, Farms, and Vineyards

Agriculture is also important to the state's economy. New York is the second-largest apple producing state in the United States. The industry supports almost 700 family orchards and accounts for close to 20,000 jobs. New York is a leader in grape production, ranking third in the nation behind California and Washington.

The state is also the third-leading producer of dairy products, producing around 12 billion pounds (5.4 billion kg) of milk per year.

Environmental Concerns

In the mid–1830s, the New York State legislature realized that it had to do something to ensure that New York City would have clean water in the years to come. Its solution was to grant the city the authority to build aqueducts—underground tunnels that carried water south to the city from reservoirs on land set aside in Westchester County. The first aqueduct was completed and put into service in 1842. In the early 1900s, that series of aqueducts was expanded to include land in the Catskills. Then, the legislature gave the city the right to purchase more land as its water needs grew. Modern-day New Yorkers benefit greatly from the foresight of politicians from an earlier day.

"One of the reasons that New York State has prospered has been its visionary investments in its future," says lawyer Jonathan Hanning. "One of those is the New York watersheds [reservoirs of clean water]."

Though a real success, the upstate watersheds policy has raised an important environmental issue: how to balance the city's need for clean water with its upstate neighbors' desire for economic development. Some citizens of New York's rural communities decided not to sell their land to the city, preferring to use it themselves to build homes and start businesses. To make matters worse for the Big Apple, upstate construction can create pollutants that run into the city's valuable water supply.

In 1992, a New York City agency called the Department of Environmental Protection, or simply the DEP, began to work with upstate farms, many of them dairy farms, in a voluntary program that offered the farmers funds and other assistance to make their farms more environmentally sound. "The hope, of course," said Larry Beckhardt, program director, "is that cleaner farms will eventually lead to a cleaner environment and cleaner water for the city." In the past two decades, the DEP has helped many farms run more efficiently and at a greater profit.

In 1997, five years after the DEP farm program began, then-Governor Pataki negotiated an agreement called the Watershed Memorandum of Agreement that forced the city to pay upstate towns for use of their land. It was an effort to address the upstaters' economic needs while allowing city residents access to clean water.

New York in the Twenty-first Century

At the end of the first decade of the twenty-first century, New York, like most states, was feeling the effects of the severe economic recession that had begun by 2008. Many people lost jobs in the banking and finance industry, an especially important one for New York's economy, as some financial firms went out of business and others suffered losses. Hundreds of billions of dollars in assistance from the U.S. government helped the financial industry recover. Workers in other fields were also hard hit by the recession.

But New York and its economy still had their traditional strengths, including one of the state's greatest resources: its people. Four hundred years after Henry Hudson, people from all over the world were still coming to New York to work hard and build a better life.

I Love New York

New York's official State Song is "I Love New York." It was written and composed by Steve Karmen in 1977.

NEW YORK
STATE MAP

Massena

Plattsburgh

St. Lawrence R.

Ogdensburg

Lake Champlain

11

Thousand Islands

11

Lake Placid

ADIRONDACK MOUNTAINS

87

81

Watertown

Long Lake

Mt. Marcy

9

Henderson Bay

Black R.

Raquette Lake

Lake George

Adirondack Park

Lake Ontario

Oswego

Oneida Lake

ADIRONDACK MOUNTAINS

4

Glens Falls

Fort Niagara State Park

Niagara Falls

Iroquois National Wildlife Refuge

Rochester

Erie Canal

490

Syracuse

90

Utica

Mohawk R.

Great Sacandaga Lake

Saratoga Springs

4

Niagara Falls

New York State Thruway

Seneca Falls

20

APPALACHIAN PLATEAU

Schenectady

Grand Island

90

20

Women's Rights National Historical Park

81

Otsego Lake

Cooperstown

National Baseball Hall of Fame

Albany

Troy

Buffalo

20A

Seneca Lake

Cayuga Lake

90

Lake Erie

Genesee R.

390

Finger Lakes

Susquehanna R.

88

CATSKILL MOUNTAINS

87

62

219

86

Ithaca

11

9

90

20

Chautauqua Lake

15

Elmira

86

Binghamton

Cannonsville Reservoir

Catskill Park

9W

Franklin D. Roosevelt Presidential Library & Museum

Jamestown

Olean

Allegany State Park

209

Delaware R.

44

Clarence Fahnestock State Park

Poughkeepsie

84

Hudson R.

6

Fishers Island

Montauk Point

Middletown

Harriman State Park

684

Long Island Sound

287

Port Chester

Long Island

Hampton Bays

95

Mount Vernon

Central Park

495

Fire Island National Seashore

Statue of Liberty National Monument

New York

Fire Island

Staten Island

Gateway National Recreation Area

ATLANTIC OCEAN

Legend

Interstate	
Major Highway	
Appalachian Trail	
City or Town	
State Capital	
Highest Point in State	
Mountains	
Historic Site	
State Forest	
National Park	
State Park	
National Wildlife Refuge	
Other Points of Interest	

N W E S

0   miles   100

NEW YORK
MAP SKILLS

1. If a person wanted to travel by boat from Buffalo to New York City, what two waterways would he or she use?

2. Which Great Lakes are located near New York?

3. What city is located at the southern end of Cayuga Lake?

4. What mountain range is located in southeastern New York?

5. What interstate runs north-south though the middle of the state?

6. What national park is located on Long Island?

7. What point of interest can you find outside of the city of Poughkeepsie?

8. What two lakes can you find in the middle of the Adirondack Mountains?

9. What interstate runs between Albany and Binghamton?

10. What is the northernmost city on this map?

Finger Lake

Allegheny State Park

Susquehanna River

1. Erie Canal and Hudson River
2. Lake Ontario and Lake Erie
3. Ithaca
4. Catskill Mountains
5. Interstate 81
6. Fire Island National Seashore
7. Franklin D. Roosevelt Presidential Library & Museum
8. Raquette and Long Lakes
9. Interstate 88
10. Massena

State Seal, Flag, and Song

The state seal includes a sunrise, a three-masted ship, and a Hudson River sloop within a shield. An eagle is perched on a globe above the shield. Below is the state's motto, "Excelsior," which means "Ever Upward" in Latin. On either side of the shield stand figures representing Liberty and Justice. The Secretary of State is the keeper of the seal, which is used to authenticate official records. The Secretary of State may authorize, or approve, the use of the seal for certain educational or commemorative purposes.

New York's flag shows the official state seal against a dark blue background. The present flag is a modern version of a Revolutionary War flag. The original is at the Albany Institute of History and Art.

To see the lyrics of the New York State Song, "I Love New York," go to **www.statesymbolsusa.org/New_York/stateSONG.html**

Glossary

American Civil War A war in the United States between the North (Union) and the South (Confederates) that took place between 1861 and 1865.

commodities Economic goods that are bought and sold, such as agricultural products, livestock, energy, and precisous metals.

confederacy A group of people brought together for a common interest or goal.

convention A meeting of persons for a common purpose.

devastating Reducing to ruin.

disaster Something that happens suddenly and causes much suffering or loss.

empire A group of regions that are controlled by one ruler or one government.

famine A great shortage of food.

immigrants People who come to a country to live there.

legislature A body of persons having the power to make laws.

minorities Parts of a population that differ from the main groups in a society in some way and are often given unfair treatment.

persecution The act of being treated continually in a way meant to be cruel or harmful.

raid A sudden attack.

restrictions Things that are kept within bounds.

significant Having much importance.

strategic Of great importance within a whole or for a planned purpose.

symphony A concert by musicians who play wind, string, and percussion instruments.

More About New York

BOOKS

Bauer, Marion Dane. *Celebrating New York*. Boston, MA: Houghton Mifflin Harcourt, 2013.

Lamprell, Klay. *Not for Parents New York City: Everything You Ever Wanted to Know*. Melbourne, Australia: Lonely Planet Publications, 2011.

Panchyk, Richard. *New York City History for Kids: From New Amsterdam to the Big Apple*. Chicago, IL: Chicago Review Press, 2012.

Staton, Hilarie. *Ellis Island*. New York, NY: Chelsea House, 2010.

Zuger, Sascha. *Moon New York*. Berkeley, CA: Avalon Travel, 2010.

WEBSITES

Get the Facts About New York State (New York State Department of State):

www.dos.state.ny.us/kids_room/index.html

New York State Government Homepage:

www.state.ny.us

Official New York State Tourism Website:

iloveny.com

ABOUT THE AUTHORS

Dan Elish is the author of many nonfiction books for young readers. He lives in New York City with his wife and their two children.

Stephanie Fitzgerald has been writing nonfiction for children for more than ten years, and she is the author of more than twenty books. Her specialties include history, wildlife, and popular culture. She lives in Stamford, Connecticut, with her husband and their daughter.

Index

Page numbers in **boldface** are illustrations.

Index